CORPORATE Non-Violence (Ahimsa)

Corporate spirituality for eternal bliss

notionpress.com

CORPORATE Non-Violence (Ahimsa)

Corporate spirituality for eternal bliss

Munnishwar Vasudeva

notionpress.com

Notion Press

Old No. 38, New No. 6

McNichols Road, Chetpet

Chennai - 600 031

First Published by Notion Press 2016

ISBN 978-93-5206-884-5

Contents

Acknowledgments

Grateful to my Mom late Satya Vasudeva and her sister late Bimla Devi who taught me how to follow religious rituals and worldly deeds without any compromise and with equal zeal.

and

Also grateful to my Dad Kharaiti Lal Vasudeva who inspired me by gifting intellectual simulating English magazine when I could not converse in English and to my maternal uncle Ramesh Datt Lakhanpal who gave me a crash course on English at an early age.

Preface

The book has been written for the corporate citizens who drive the world's economy. A lot of effort has been put to understand religions like Christianity, Islam, Hinduism and Buddhism and drive conclusions on the cultural influences. Culture greatly influences the corporate outcomes, which are driven by its corporate citizens. Religious beliefs are still present in corporate citizens because of their cultural upbringing, which has its share of religious influences.

The book has aimed to bring about positive influences of ahimsa or nonviolence taught by all religions and culture directly or indirectly. In today's competition, all citizens are stressed out. This book helps corporate citizens to destress and live a peaceful life.

Corporate duties of the citizens help them to fantasize about achieving spirituality in exactly the same way as those in medieval times when the society was less complex and the citizens devoted most of their time on spiritual efforts.

Most of the writings that have been shared in this book are author's experiments with principles of corporate ahimsa as a corporate citizen in his professional career spread over three decades.

PART ONE
Journey to Maturity

1 Culture Intrinsically Imbibed from Religious Beliefs

Though circumstantial upbringing does influence one's culture, religious influence is more permanent. All the epic historic wars were fought and have been influenced by culture based on religious beliefs. During most of the epic wars, there were three types of careers: warriors, priests and peasants. All these careers were influenced by the country's religion. The country slowly evolved into a well-defined, technically competent one. Germany, France, United Kingdom and United States are the best countries that manufacture defense equipment. All the big ticket inventions are from these countries. In the *Gospel of Truth*, Jesus inspired and taught his followers to be the best artisans and to gain domain knowledge in forgery, architecture and so on.

The rest of the world like Saudi Arabia and the Middle East gained expertise in trading. This is where Islam originated. Prophet Mohammad's initial years were spent learning trading. Latin America and the European Union remained agriculture-based economies as Jesus preached let food grains be served to the communities that need it most. The Asian continent had influences of Christianity and Islam because of various invasions and later slowly came to terms with their religious influences of Buddhism and Hinduism, leading them to gain expertise in agriculture and tourism. In India, the Hindu God, Lord Krishna, conveyed the message in the form of Bhagavad Gita, which preached self-realization and selfless service to the society. Gautama Buddha preached self-realization to attain nirvana and good rebirth.

As all these four religions evolved and spread across the world and had its cultural influences in the changing world as the countries chose democracies to monarchy. Industrialization in European Union, United States and Latin America strengthened the cooperative agricultural economy. However, in Asia there was food grains revolution and Saudi Arabia/ Middle East became a strong trading hub. African countries remained underdeveloped as religious preaching reached very late.

Whatever transition took place in the countries, the big motivation factor was the religion of the region that influenced the cultural change as well.

Today, the world is best known as a single global market because of faster mobility due to air travels, but IT revolution has its own impact on the cultural changes as knowledge is shared instantly and is not dependent on physical mobility. The best of all cultures could be learnt and adapted very fast creating new kind of cross-breed cultures enriching the global market.

2 Inspirations from Great Leaders

The best-known leaders who were freedom fighters and civil right activists are Martin King Luther Jr., Nelson Mandela, Mahatma Gandhi and so on and they are well known for their nonviolence or ahimsa methods. Everybody should be inspired by these leaders for their ahimsa-based methods and selfless services for their fellow citizens.

Just try to imagine why these leaders helped for the cause of humanity. Think about their motivation; despite knowing that they will suffer they still did what they thought was good for their countries. They did it to make human lives better.

Read biographies of famous people who follow ahimsa or see their movies and you will understand the messages of unity. Mortal soul when enlightened can become a pied piper. It can also be perceived that the leaders converted religious connotations into motivational political deliberations to awaken humankind.

Just try to imagine the mortals who listened to immortals like Jesus, Krishna, Buddha or Prophet Mohammad. What would have happened to them? These mortals would be enjoying the Bliss of God's palace.

Nobody can deny the fact that these leaders would have attained salvation. If that is correct, then it should not be doubted that the followers of the leaders who strive to bring the desired change can also attain salvation.

It is conclusive that if leaders are important for the cause, then the followers who are sincere are equally important as it is they who are the medium of change for the good of mankind.

Now, just imagine these leaders reborn on earth. How would they motivate us to do the right thing as per today's relevance? Ahimsa would be the best relevant message that would be repeated.

3 Grounded Realities of Life

The messengers of God did not preach the mankind in luxury. They suffered to take out the sufferings of the mankind to build comfortable futures. Sufferings, if one may call it, are inevitable and are integral part of life cycles.

The percentage share of natural resources per person is shrinking day by day that makes the whole society very competitive. This kind of competition to get more shares of natural resources leads to society's temptation to join the rat race.

Only 1% population of the world owns 75% wealth, whereas the rest 99% fight for 25% of the wealth. This wealth gap might increase in future making the 99% population vulnerable. So the ground reality is to live life to be a part of 1% club or survive the vulnerability of 99% club. In either case, one needs to focus on fair means to achieve the goal. Distractions are too many, shortcut temptations are too many but long-tested treaded path eventually gets you what you want that you deserve with dignity and be blessed. The path is ahimsa with a sentence "love thy neighbor before thyself." All religions teach this common fundamental belief.

The gap of 75:25 vs. 1:99 was always there. It is not this century's process but existed since humankind existed. Earlier, the kings owned the kingdom; today, smart entrepreneurs without coronation own large amounts of wealth. Ninety-nine percent of people aspire to become wealthy owners of a company, with a sense of inspiration to adopt dignified fair means for a successful career. Life styles have changed, surroundings have changed and the only constants are honesty, dexterity, ahimsa, selfless service and so on. These factors cannot be removed from people's lives, though the percentages of these constants have varied. These factors have helped societies move forward on solid footings.

4 Inspirations of Childhood Memories

Humankind is blessed with short memories but childhood memories are more or less inscribed in the heart and remain till the end. Nature has blessed us to remember mostly the positive memories. It is strange but it is a fact with certain exceptions.

A lot of risk-taking activities are learnt during childhood because of blessings of ignorance. The naughtier the one is during the childhood, the better and blessed is the person who treads a most adventurous career. Protective kids though makes their parents proud of highest grades but timidly struggle in life and circumvent decisions.

The degree of risk taken by today's kids has drastically reduced due to overprotective parents who unintentionally suppress the kid's learning process of risk taking. Earlier, parents could not afford gadgets but today they are in abundance and driving the kids indoor, and parents feel very safe about kids using gadgets. Earlier, grannies and grandpas used to answer the inquisitive innocent queries of the kids and these were inspired from traditional fairy tales. Earlier, the parents did extraordinary services to their kids or grandkids by sharing the childhood stories of messengers of God. Today, grannies and grandpas have been replaced by search engines.

Wish kids learnt a lesson from the fairy tale where a giant demon was killed by a stone; when all the villagers thought that the demon was too big to kill, a kid innocently told them that he was too big not to miss.

Wish kids listened to a story about a snake charmer who left his kid sleeping under the supervision of a mongoose. When he came back he saw the blood on mongoose's mouth and killed it thinking that it had killed the kid. He later saw that the mongoose had killed the snake, thereby saving the kid. What a lesson to grow up with!

There are certain things that we used to do when we were kids. These are luxuries for today's kids. They rarely, if at all, do these activities: climbing a tree, crossing the road, going to school on a cycle without supervision, traveling alone in a train or bus, waking up early by the chirping sounds of the birds, eating guava or any other fruit by plucking it from the tree, playing with street dogs, saying hello to a stranger, patiently listening to granny's stories at bedtime, sharing a chocolate with another kid, going to all places of worship irrespective of one' own faith, playing in the summer noon, splashing water on the streets during rainy days, joy riding on a stray donkey and so on. Oh my God, the kids are deprived of these fundamental rights, which could shape their future better and make it more fascinating.

Earlier, any kid who was feeling hungry and without pocket money used to feel that it was his or her right to steal his or her friend's food or barge into any neighbor's house. Such a kid was simply called a naughty kid. Today, kids can never imagine stealing things and know that they will be called thieves. This transformation has made today's generation very reserved and selfish; by not asking or giving a helping hand when they grow up.

Parents, even if deprived of great childhood memories, should make sure that kids grow up in harmony with nature as much as possible without the fear of getting hurt physically or mentally. The childhood memories should be relished by one and all.

5 Fond Memories of Educating Oneself

How difficult it is as a kid to leave the company of his mother who is the first teacher and attend the first formal teaching class. Just remember how the mother pushes her dearest to the school by pampering the innocent soul with the tastiest food in the lunch box. The taste of food from the first lunch box lingers on in one's life and the first lesson of life is learnt "sacrifice of love for the good of dear ones." Mother, the greatest teacher teaches us.

By attending the first class and making a lot of new acquaintances, the kid becomes impatient to grow up and just wants to take a leap and become a senior student of his school. All the school grades are forgotten while growing up. Only summer holidays remain very close to the heart. For holidaying, traveling across the country and the continents meeting new people and watching exotic locations matures the kid to a different level. Fondness for nature's beauty, reading books and listening to the music seeps in at this stage.

Parents do take the opportunity of holidaying by taking kids to the places of worship of historical importance. The learning phase of religions does happen at this stage. Decoding the cultural differentiation, which may be mature or immature does happen as well.

Wish at this stage one had spent a few days of the holidays in the countryside, on the shore of a river, climbing a tough mountain terrain, enjoying the beauty of the forest. Wish one had seen how the food grains, vegetable and fruits are grown in the fields. How the growers look after their produce? Just uproot a carrot, wash it and eat it, you will feel like you are eating a divine food. Just pluck ladyfingers, cook it on the field and taste it, you will realize that this fresh vegetable from the field tastes much better than what you are eating in your home with the best condiments. Just pluck a corn cob from a plant and eat it and you will realize it to be the sweetest cob you have eaten ever. Similarly try eating a guava, a mango and it will stump you. Countryside experience of watching agronomical activities will enrich you and make you appreciate the disciplined approach for getting a good harvest. This is tougher than educating oneself through books.

Just visit any farmer's house and request him for food or beg for it even if you have to. Just taste the food you will feel it is better than having food in the best restaurants in the cities.

Wish one goes for a picnic on the river shore. One should also experience cooking for it. You should take a bath in the flowing river to freshen up. You should eat the food that would taste much better than your first lunch box, and also would make you feel that that you are the best chef in the world. You should definitely try your luck at catching a fish. If you end up lucky, whether you cook it right or not, you would just love it.

Besides getting grades in your classes' exposure to new locations, intermixing with new people, experimenting something unconventional brings a lot of new learning and helps build the character and self-confidence as well.

Progression from innocent childhood phase to the educating phase is the best phase of the life. This transition phase shapes the cultural maturity of a person, which is influenced by inherited religious beliefs, circumstances and education. At this stage, still the malleability of mind and soul helps in maintaining the state of optimism. A metamorphic change of the next phase of life determines if one remains in a state of elasticity or plasticity.

6 Initial Inhibitions of Professional Life

The first lunch box of this stage does not have a mom's inspiring love and affection as one just enters the world of jungle or a battle field. This is a lonely journey where one starts picking new family members.

The newcomers have an introductory session with seniors and super bosses and there might be awkward moments during this session. The most awkward moments may be when trying to shake hands with reluctant seniors. Saying hello instead of good afternoon or buenos dias and so on invites glares instead of smiles. One must feel really lucky if these two moments are not faced. Celebrations of the first day at the job over a couple of drinks result in a very serious introspection. Ideas like visiting places of worship or seeking blessings of the parents occur to bring some extra luck for the not so good first day at the job.

In awe, new corporate citizens start working toward enriching cultural exchanges. New terms like selfless community service as an alternate to visiting places of worships, taking solace from seeking blessings from parents, seeking forgiveness from your college mates, reading relevant holy book and so on are learnt. With a new zeal, the journey is taken up.

Casual approach of education days now looks like to be a luxury. Sensibilities once blissfully ignored start making sense, words like thank you, I am terribly sorry, Salud/God bless, pleasure to meet you, may I help you and so on. Lunch session in the office becomes very suffocating as real hunger is taken over by looking at who is eating what and how much. First time a thought crosses the mind wishing to be the last man in the canteen for a carefree lunch to satiate.

Although the pain of separation during birth time due to umbilical cord separation is not remembered, hunger pains become overpowering in an office atmosphere making a rebirth (in a corporate sector) without any cries.

Interactions with colleagues, seniors, customers and so on with diverse backgrounds make learning either interesting or painful. One treads this path without much choice as the main focus is surviving the tides of corporate childhood.

Invisible and invincible war on efficiency is being fought that is bloodless but very violent. This unintentional violent war germinates from the seeds of miscommunications and wrong body language – bad choice of basic words like saying thanks instead of sorry and vice versa. A smile instead of emotive expressions chiseled the corporate weapons of its citizens. Simple incidents taken seriously create the aura of hardcore corporate journey, which is very long and tiring unless one wants to make it interesting and enjoyable.

The corporate childhood journey does start with the lessons learnt from leaders like Gandhi and Mandela. A decision is taken at this stage on whether to persist with good learning like ahimsa or struggle like a warrior. It is quite tough to decide but the taste of blood leads the majority of corporate citizens to become warriors. The fact remains that unintentional mistakes inhibiting from the lack of maturity change most of our cultural values.

7 Learning from Religious Books like Holy Bible, Holy Koran, Bhagavad Gita and Tipitaka

We should read holy books to be religious or the religion expects everyone to read holy books – this is like the chicken and egg situation. Chanting at religious places with rituals of offering is what religion means to most of us. Parents simply order their kids to follow the rituals and show them the ways without even reading the messages of the Holy books.

Successful corporate citizens live with a notion of getting the blessings of their parents and others feel that their parents should have performed religious rituals properly. The fact remains that unintentional mistakes of the parents do get passed over to the growing kids. This shackles the conscience of the poor soul when in trouble.

Do not worry about the ritualistic discipline of reading a Holy book, just read the book the way it could be comfortably read at a convenient time. Buy the translations of the Holy book if the original is not understood. Reading the book will answer all your questions. The best lesson is to follow the instructions of the God. This experience will soothe you and will remove the burden, which was in fact superficial.

Well, if reading the Holy book is a difficult proposition, then find a suitable mentor to help through tough times. The movie "Scent of a Women" is a good movie. Charlie, a boy, finds guidance from a Colonel Frank. If a kind colonel could not be found, then visit an Old Age Home and talk to some senior citizen and listen to their advice.

Simple religious readings even for pleasure are better than reading a thrilling novel. It is worth a shot that the only thing is that you just have to believe Him at least till the time you are reading it. Do not worry about Him. Let Him worry about you. Just follow what He has conveyed in these religious books.

To be a good corporate citizen, just try reading religious books, any religious book, which will give a thoughtful insight or understanding of all kinds of cultures and will help achieve a formidable corporate team par excellence. In the process, the team shall overtake the team leader proving that corporate citizens are more important.

Words like honesty, integrity, see no evil, hear no evil, truth, help others before self and so on will start making sense. This will make one's corporate journey very lively and exciting – as exciting as a kid going on a school trip.

PART TWO

Taking Clues from One's Surroundings

1 Learning from Family and Neighbors

Family members are blood relations not by choice, where their numbers are decided irrespective of genders. Designations change with every new addition. Man becomes husband, woman becomes wife and further additions to the family make them maa or paa. Additions to families bring tough responsibilities. “Spiderman” type of responsibility means “with great powers come greater responsibility” – “Spiderman” is not a real person, only a fictional character. A lot of hard work is expected in the corporate environment.

Growing up with a family, a subconscious realm is observed in a mirror with a flashback. A flashback expresses that the good phase of childhood was better than college days and romantic days were better than the marriage. The lure of good days though quite fictional had to be forgotten taking pride in new designations.

Attending office, returning home, attending to a crying baby the whole night, reluctantly going to the office and rushing back home to see the baby’s smile are very satisfying in one's life. The smile of the baby precedes one's tiredness making this journey one of self-exploration and very gratifying. The new role in a family is well deserved. One should thank God for His blessings and one must realize that when it was the first time under distress no prayers were performed but still a blissful smile was showered.

A refreshing lesson is learnt while earning a smile on the face of the dear little one, which brings eternal joy. This gives a feeling of a job well done.

Overwhelming emotions outweigh any material gains when a simple word like maa/paa is heard. One relieves the childhood, school days all over again maturing to learn the hard facts of life, which do add a lot of value to corporate cultures.

The word "neighbor" is redefined to include neighbors and the corporate neighbors; a friend in need is a friend indeed and when in distress unsolicited help is considered as an angelic help. Little gestures like thank you, may I help you, count on me and so on become religious rhyme and these were taught once upon a time by granny. Lessons are learnt as a kid and used now in the corporate field.

While leaving home in a good mood, the neighbor's kids are observed to be fighting, which is an unimaginative scene where someone gets killed, and upon return to home the same kids are playing together, which is a near imaginative scene. A wishful desire creeps in mind to make friends with the disgruntled colleague but alas the ego becomes a slippery road with a lot of bumpers and the wonderful transformed scene of the kids playing after a fight becomes a blurred dream.

Granny's stories are inspiring and are revisited when parents almost force kids to congratulate the winning neighbor's kid. Granny's short stories are put to the test by corporate citizens with some success and sometimes with bitterness but still worth experimenting.

2 Inspirations from Film Songs, Gazals and Films

In a successful career, inspiration is almost nonexistent or rare because satisfaction measurements are dynamic and ever changing. A struggling career doesn't help a corporate citizen to take a clue from the world leaders like Gandhi, Mandela and Martin Luther King Jr; not even the struggles of Jesus, Prophet Mohammad, Krishna or Buddha come to one's mind because of the complexity of today's materialism.

Great movies are made about great people. However, movies like Spiderman, Cinderella's man, Gandhi, The Da Vinci's Code, Gladiator, Robin Hood, The Patriot, The Help and The Bucket List are based on fiction and these movies can also be inspirational. Corporate citizens can be inspired to sacrifice for the society, to help thy brothers, to follow nonviolence, to understand that forgiveness is far more powerful than vengeance and so on.

All these great movies have different narrations and end up conveying messages that the Messengers of God had delivered a few centuries ago. Imagine the script writer convincing the producer about the worthiness of making the movie. Also imagine a producer finding a director and trusting the script that leads to all the actors and technicians joining hands. After spending millions on the movie and enjoying the work, a positive message is conveyed, which is inspiring. Whatever unconventional or out of the box ideas may be thought for depicting inspiration nothing could be invented beyond the messages of the Messengers of God. Learn from these movies and adapt good corporate practices for one's own good.

Listen to songs or gazals from any region of any genre. In a receptive environment a lot of positive experience is gained. Majority of songs are romantic, which may be sad or jovial, and ends in a positive note blessing the other side. These romantic songs may inspire us to romanticize corporate deeds, thereby making life's journey a romantic one and a so-called success or failure becomes just incidental. A good positive song can have a calming effect and heal one's soul.

Try to decode any instant hit popular song that crosses the cultural, regional and language barriers. The result is due to the hard work of a music director and lyricist, only a few initial lines of the song are remembered. Try to analyze the efforts that have made this song famous, touching so many hearts. The reason most likely is going to be a team effort, where members are of a diversified cultural background. The team cannot single out a specific reason for the success of the song. One thinks it is divine intervention?

Just try to feel the height of innocence in a movie "life of PI" when the central character thanks his God by saying "thanks Vishnu for introducing me to Jesus." Anyone who had written this dialog is worth a million blessings.

3 Be Spiritual if You Can

The definition of spirituality "instincts gained from religious practices," or "a faculty of reason now surpassed by the faculty of intuition." Spirituality can be replaced by gaining instincts of religious teachings and that is the beauty of spirituality. It is difficult to understand if one can be spiritual without following religious practices. Spirituality can still be achieved without religious reading as long as one's existence prevails in loving one's own deeds. The deeds are loving your family, loving animals, loving neighbors, loving and caring for your surroundings, taking pride in helping others, loving what you do to feed your family and taking a share of global wealth. Loving all these is also equally religious if not the same.

Reading mysticism, the theology of most of faith, a derivative could be arrived at by assuming God's presence and His blessings in one's good deeds. Another very important factor in gaining spirituality is passion. If one is passionate to help others selflessly, it could be termed as a spiritual deed. Loving your job and performing the actions for achieving corporate goal could also be termed as a spiritual deed. This spiritual deed indeed could be a beginning of salvation as well.

Transcendence of cultural values and having the invisible coating of principles of faith is spirituality in itself. It is a matter of choice to choose spirituality or materialism. The fact is that spirituality has a bonus, which is materialism. The materialism has a bonus of repentance. The songs, the films, the world leaders preaching and so on are giving this hint so either regret learning to live for a lesson or simply believe this. The choice is simple, be spiritual if you can.

The definition of Forbidden Apple has not still changed but its identification has been blurred. Admiring a beauty in a beauty is spiritual but lusting for the beauty is materialism. Thus, spirituality cannot be simpler than this. The difficult part of spirituality worth trying without compulsion is to be *indifferent to the success and failure*. Exercising this may be of medicinal value.

Religious readings are stagnant and ever evolving to be complex but spirituality becomes simpler with the times. The principle of nonviolence has somehow survived as a basic premise of faith and spirituality.

If religious and spiritual gurus are inspired to attain salvation, then corporate citizens with good deeds can also be inspired, otherwise He shall be alone in His Kingdom. If a man is selfish, so is He.

4 Learn Spirituality from The Dog

If one is required to identify the man's loyal friend, the first name that comes to mind is the dog. Man likes dogs, but many dislike dog. Still the loyalist friend of a man is a dog.

If society has evolved appreciating dog's loyalty, a desire is necessitated to decode the dog's behavior, which may be perceived to be spiritual. His Master's Voice the Dog is spiritual and may be a bit of an exaggeration but its actions are worth noticing to be spiritual.

Just observe a dog in a pet shop, see how the dog interacts with the humans. All the buyers who went shopping for a pet do not always buy the pet, but the dog sells itself with an attitude, which can put the best salesman of the world to shame. An interviewer can learn a few points from dog behavior. A disgruntled corporate citizen can have a great idea to connect to the boss. The fact is that it has chosen him/her not otherwise is a lesson in itself that could be the beginning of the spirituality.

Just like humanity got instructions from the heavens about what to do and what not to do, a dog also gets a routine set of instructions from the master. Dogs never forget their master's rules. The dogs obey the disciplines in a specified time with innocent gestures of pleading.

The spiritual lessons from the dog are many, but few are worth sharing: gestures after it is been fed a morsel. The gesture doesn't require any language it is universally understood. Master is happy, the dog is happy. Master is upset, the dog is upset. Master is playful, the dog is playful. Master scolds the dog with or without a reason but the dog is never upset for long. Just try to visualize these situations by changing the role of a dog and let the master be either God himself, the boss, the wife, sibling, kids, neighbors and so on and let nothing but love emanate all over. There will not be any need for memory pills. The word ego will disappear from the dictionary. Ego disappears and spirituality sets in.

It is strange that movies are only about genetically mutated spiders and lizards and not about a dog. Probably, the barking of a dog is negative but it must be understood that it is the only audible way of communication. The dog is best understood and admired and its beautiful gestures are a very nice way of communication. As a parent, it is good to adopt dogs to teach kids about responsibility. Return on investment on the dog from here is as a parent in corporate world self-correction will happen as a default because the spirituality is contagious.

Obedience is a form of spirituality, which the dog has, a learning on this aspect for actualization for every day deeds bring in harvest more than required.

5 Go the Extra Mile to Help Others

The evolution of mankind from Stone Age to democracy has witnessed a lot of bloodshed that led to hard learned lesson of brotherhood or "serve others before self." Transition from bartering of goods to the currency exchanges transformed the nations toward the material greed. A lot of formal inventions happened during the advent of the democracies, which really helped society flourish. Inventions like automobile, farm mechanization, airplane, Internet helped reduce the distances between two cities and brought new cultural dynamics.

In the name of career and ambition, a lot of values are unintentionally forgotten. Definition of contentment like "one is contented when one is as grateful for pain as for the pleasure" had lost its shine and is not even paraphrased at any platform of communication. Inevitably cultural values, which had the encapsulation of religion, are now coated with a lot of materialism. This has resulted in corporate citizens into becoming beautiful wolves. These beautiful wolves are called leaders in the corporate and the corporate citizen survival is much more challenging than ever before. The messiahs or leaders are now rare who save herds of sheep from the wolves, so sheep are on their own. There is no self-exploration today to identify oneself as a wolf or a sheep.

Corporate citizen's survival (or a sheep) can take a clue from the trade evolution of bartering of goods to trading in currency. If you had helped, you shall be helped. Help others in need and others will help you when you are in need. If trading in currency holds good today, then bartering a help also holds true even today. The only difference between the two is that the condition does not apply to bartering as it is not time bound and may have many returns.

Visualize a pearl found in a shell by a deep sea diver. It is useless till someone makes a beautiful necklace and sells it. Just keep in mind that all pearls collected do not fit in a necklace as some are hard to pierce.

Fishing for a living is not a one man's job, it is a team work – a fishnet expert, boat man, a diver, fish segregator, salesman and so on. A good catch does not mean a good earning till the catch is sold; a good catch will be of lesser value unless it is segregated properly.

Today's corporate expectations from corporate citizens work more or less in a manner that is comparable to the pearl and fishing business. All citizens are interdependent for survival. Helping each other is the way out for survival. Helping without expectations or selfless help is much spicier.

It is like the chicken and egg situation that a corporate citizen is happy in his family life because of corporate world or vice versa. It is not difficult to conclude that it is in the interest of a corporate citizen to be happy at his corporate environment to make his family happy. Happiness is not the choice but a compulsion that is based on basic rules of cultural wisdom. The wisdom is based on insights of learning from the films, good poetry, neighbors, kids and so on. The best and the easiest is to barter help for help and strengthen it to go extra miles on it.

I felt a sense of achievement when my kid smiled and when my colleague in corporate world conveyed gratitude upon a promotion or a raise. Experiencing this gratitude cleanses one's heart and soul as it promotes a feeling of a sense of achievement. One will never trade this gesture at any cost as it is a lifetime medallion longing for more embellishments.

6 Intermixing of all Types of Religious and Regional Fellow Global Citizens

Globally, the races had attained unique competencies and blending these competencies has made the world a more beautiful place to live in. This blending is in fact an interaction of global citizens of all kinds of religion and regions.

The relevance of today's world economy in the absence of the historical imperialism of various empires is difficult to visualize in the right prospective. Imperialism was brutal but it had consequences in shaping the countries stronger. The consequences could be measured by observing the countries like China ruled by Japanese, commonwealth countries by Britishers, invasion on the United States by Britishers, Saudi Arabia ruling Spain, French ruling West Africa and so on. The main consequence was the intermixing of good values of regions and religion. History has taught us that the transgression of the regions was not so bad.

In the past, the overflowing aggressive energy of the youth was for fighting wars but in the later centuries it was toward competitive international sports. Winning medals for the country made more sense than dying for the country fighting unending wars. Changing this attitude by the international community is much more laudable as the aggressive energy was channelized in productive ways. People with different religious beliefs came together and competed in sports. The ultimate spoils of war – the desire of three Ws (wine, women and wealth) – for winning the wars is the same as that for winning the competition so that the sports could sustain the competiveness even today.

Conceptualizing the legal residential emigration helped people to cross borders for the sake of sports (or intellectual) and this broke the shackles of the saturated limits. The sporting records are broken in every event for centuries, if technology is responsible so is the cultural intermixing based on regions and religions as well. The power of innovation is seen as a result of this intermixing.

Professional sporting events like IPL, International Premier League, and NBA, National Basketball Association, which has a mix of players from different nationalities, prove this point further. Freshness from regions and religions adds flavor in the game but most importantly the new levels of innovations break the barrier of competencies. The effect of the intermixing will be achieved in the corporate world, enriching the citizens and helping the corporate achieve a great deal of excellence.

Hollywood film industry is another example of pushing the limits of arts with a good blend of regions and religions. A good example could be taken from the movie Gandhi. A tall Indian figure Mohandas Karamchand Gandhi was best played by a non-Indian Ben Kingsley, produced and directed by a Britisher Richard Attenborough, music was by an Indian Pundit Ravi Shankar and so on. Similar success stories of great movies could be explored based on the right kind of a blend.

Different regions bring unique experience of hardships to the team and the religion and culture flavor the team work with optimism. The blend of religion and region make life's journey an interesting one.

Gandhi adapted Jesus' preaching during the freedom struggles for India. Gandhi started a nonviolence movement by saying "if someone slaps you on one cheek, offer him your other cheek." For caste divided Indians, Gandhi adapted Jesus' miracles curing the leprosy patients. Gandhi made untouchability a morale crime. A Hindu adapted to the teachings of the Bible and integrated regions and religions. There is no better example than this that would help motivate all the corporate citizens to adapt for one's own good.

7 Believe in Astrology if You Want To

A lot of findings have been collated by studying the movement of moon, sun and the planets. The cosmic movements are correlated with the time and place of birth to predict the destiny. In the past, kings and queens used to consult astrologers to ask about the outcome of war, the gender of their heirs and life span. Kingdoms used to choose the heirs born under auspicious astrological signs. Astrology was a closely held secret of the rich but eventually it became accessible to everybody.

Astrologers have extended their discoveries to predict love life, compatibility in marriage, career progression, health issues, property disputes, gambling and so on. The success rate of the predictions is relatively high but it still cannot be taken as a perfect forecast. Sometimes astrological forecasts really help. A blind faith in it is preposterous.

In today's rat race, temptations are too many to trust the astrology as the race is inching very close among the corporate citizens. Everyone feels that they are not the lesser of Gods but why someone else is more successful further assist the astrology to flourish. The comparisons are avoidable in the corporate world. It has a bad tendency to distrust its own diligence.

It is possible to take advantage of astrology and predictions. For example, if the forecast is on ill health and an active lifestyle is recommended, then avoid junk food, get rid of the addictions and so on. If compatibility troubles in marriage at the midlife are predicted, then romance your wife once more, build more transparent love and affections and so on. If a midcareer crisis is predicted, then raise the bar on obedience toward boss and peers, work diligently and so on. If property disputes are predicted, be more conscious and explore more options to avoid any litigation.

Treat astrological prediction just like a gambler inspecting the horses before betting on the jockey. A strong man is not the one who boosts his strengths but acknowledges his weaknesses. Astrology could be a handy tool to identify the weaknesses and work on them. Let astrology be a science to take advantage of.

PART THREE

Be a Good Corporate Citizen

Let there be fresh air circulation in our stuffy culture and thrive for a peaceful coexistence. If the messiahs and their messages conveyed to the mankind were a Godly act, then followers of these messages are equally important. Followers taking lessons from *Journey to Maturity* and taking clues from one's surroundings can also reach Him.

1 What is Ahimsa

Gandhi invented the concept as a tool for fighting freedom struggles against British rule in India. Ahimsa proved to be such a sharp sword that the Britishers had to leave India. Ahimsa had a premise of noncooperation that was just like a bloodless coup. Gandhi's actions in freedom movements had a lot of inspirations from Bible. Jesus had conveyed that those who live by swords shall die by swords. Gandhi realized this when he had to face the brunt of partition violence, then he followed ahimsa "love thy neighbors before thyself" and "see no evil and do no evil."

Two forms of ahimsa still have relevance in today's context at a global level. Government employees or the general public pressing for a demand follow ahimsa to participate in noncooperation. In the corporate world, ahimsa means prejudice-free cooperation for a good teamwork. Corporate ahimsa could be the best thing for corporate and its citizens for a win–win situation.

An embodiment in nonprejudice ahimsa was celibacy where all the humans become brothers and sisters to wed a common cause of the society. Gandhi made freedom from Britishers the common cause. The common cause for corporate ahimsa on today's pretext can be a competitive corporate.

The idea of ahimsa cannot be boxed into a single religion or culture ideals. Just like Gandhi being a Hindu he borrowed a lot of ideas from Bible, the same could have ideas from Islam, Buddhism and so on. Gandhi did not spread the religion but made it a movement in a spiritual form. Not everyone can become Gandhi but many can follow him without being shamed as a Gandhian to make one's own life worthwhile.

The idea of ahimsa is everywhere. The basics were written down in the religious books and elaborated in practical ways by the world leaders. On a corporate context, the ahimsa as an idea is elaborated in the following pages:

- Have you ever been to a location where tribes are living for many centuries? Their rituals, cultures and standard of living never change. Any rationales in what they do for a living may not make sense but one may realize that the tribes do not want to change for the fear of been changed and they are happy within the ways and means of their existence. Any kind of transgression into their culture is brutally revolted as any change in their status quo is inextricable.

Now try to emulate the tribes living in corporate world totally isolated from any kind of influences and still be progressive. The situation is a kind of vicarious immortality. The only constant in the world is change and the opposite is to live a contended life like a tribe. In a corporate world there could be a lot of nicely dressed tribesmen.

In the world of coexistence with a lot of difference of opinions in the religious beliefs, it is the culture, which binds us all together. Culture filters a lot of unnecessary religious dissimilarities. The first ahimsa principle is to be proud of one's culture with a sense of pride and respect other cultures that in turn add value to the ethical diversity. Words like Inshallah, Salud, God Bless, Namaste and so on are used in corporate conversations unifying its citizens. More exciting words are in the pipeline to spread universal ethics reinforcing the corporate ahimsa.

Religious encapsulated cultures can best be used in corporate world for career progression.

✦ Leaders like Gandhi, Mandela, Martin Luther King Jr. have not only lead the societies for a wonderful living but lit lots of undistinguishable candles that still guide mankind. Candles like quotable quotes, "The weak can never forgive. Forgiveness is the attribute of the strong," "See the good in people and help them," "Be congruent, be authentic, be your true self," "A no uttered from the deepest conviction is better than a Yes uttered merely to please or worse to avoid trouble" by **Gandhi**.

Mandela's quotes, "Man's goodness is a flame that can be hidden but never extinguished," "A good head and a good heart is always a formidable combination," "It always seems impossible until it's done," "Everyone can raise above their circumstances and achieve success if they are dedicated to and passionate about what they do."

Martin Luther King Jr. quotes, "The time is always right to do what is right," "I have decided to stick to love. Hate is too great a burden to bear," "We must live together like brothers or perish as fools," "Life's most persistent and urgent question is what are you doing for others?"

Dalai Lama, "This is my simple religion. There is no need for temples; no need for complicated philosophy. Our own brain, our own heart is our temple; the philosophy is kindness," "Our purpose in life is to help others. And if you cannot help them, at least do not hurt them," "If you want others to be happy, practice compassion. If you want to be happy, practice compassion."

One need not be a sensory expert to smell a wonderful aroma of ahimsa virtues of quotes of these great leaders. If these quotes could raise the enthusiasm of the public to struggle and conquer, then the same can be adapted by the corporate citizens to enrich their lives. Selective edition of the quotes from the leaders has condiments like love, helping others, good heart, goodness, dedication, passion, forgiveness and so on, if blended appropriately this makes a perfect spice that is universally accepted as corporate ahimsa.

Spice up corporate career by following the great leaders preaching that will never let anyone down

- Contentment in life is an impossibility. The existence of this word in the dictionary is highly questionable. Even a monk is not content till he either finds himself or Him or Moksha. Communism cannot be His idea to decide upon the Moksha, reincarnation, place in Hell or Heavens. He shall observe who is following His standard operating procedures (SOPs) without any distractions: to decide upon the fates of so many. The fact remains that competitiveness is the basic premise of the existence even He cannot avoid. He loves capitalism of good deeds in a man's life to grant what he deserves. Even God can't afford to be communist.

  Socialism having capitalism as its byproduct is here to stay for long. This is a harsh reality that holds true in a corporate environment. Under the circumstances inevitably the rat race is the key word. Surviving within this grounded reality, a path needs to be chosen. A wrong choice to reach the right path is one path. Praying for rains and you will get mud too is another one. It is a difficult choice but choices need to be taken carefully. Everyone has a choice. It is the choice, which defines oneself.

The toughest part of corporate life is to synchronize the divine SOP with the corporate SOP. To be a good corporate citizen synchronization of SOPs should be close to distinction levels. To attain the distinction level, ahimsa is the driving force, which allows a cover for the mistakes and mushrooms other quality traits for corporate success.

Be a capitalist of compiling good deeds to enjoy a blissful corporate journey.

✦ As a kid one feels a great urge to become adult and independent, but after becoming an adult everyone wants to go back to the days of the childhood. This psyche holds true in all generations of the mankind. A kid's attitude is taken as a physical form when it is an attitude. Anyone longing to remain a kid forever needs to have few effervescent attitudes appreciating the aging of the body.

The root causes of all corporate politics are group discussions over some presentations. Though a platform should be used to thrash out all the differences, the differences are not bridged, rather they are widened. Bloodless war starts from here and sheep becomes wolf and vice versa. The situation should trigger ahimsa to normalize the situation for the better of all. The initiative could be taken by a sheep or a wolf but the onus is on the sheep to bring back the wolf into sheep.

Put yourself in a situation and learn from a kid's attitude; there is no fear of rejection to say sorry and repeat it even if the sorry is superfluous. Have patience till the sorry is reciprocated with an apology giving a platform to thrash out the differences. A kid does not have any ego because of the blessing of innocence. Why can't the same enthusiasm of innocence be tested in the corporate environment when the returns are far greater? Just try to relive childhood innocence.

Another innocence of the childhood could also be tools of ahimsa like eating from the lunch box of a colleague, being the first person to congratulate upon someone's good news, to offer sincere selfless help, to lift the mood in case of a sad event and so on. Time spent on these small steps for ahimsa is valuable that even money cannot buy. These childish gestures of gratitude come from the heart and have a great degree of success rate that coalesce the corporate citizens without the help of any leadership. After all kids don't care for any kind of cloying attachment to the sense of guilt.

Adapting a childish attitude as an extension of ahimsa will never let anyone down in the Corporate World

- In reality, initial years in the corporate world are like undergraduate experience. The difference is in corporate; one is paid even for mistakes and learning. These years are receptive as those in the college days. In college days, one invests on one's education and the corporate invests in grooming the talent for futures returns.

School and college days shape the characteristics of the citizens just as a raw molded clay pot that needs to be heated for shaping it as a beautiful piece of art. This happens in the initial years of the corporate career. The amount of fire needed to shape the clay art is compared to the amount of fire that the citizen can withstand in the initial corporate years. The degree of fire defines a weak or strong character of the corporate citizen.

School and college days take a "yes" and "no" on a face value without any prejudices. This continuity needs to be maintained to follow the path of corporate ahimsa. One should have short-term memories for any kind of negativities and long sweet memories for positivity.

Make friends passionately as made in college days even during corporate journey, which is the wisest investment with assured returns.

- The maturity gained during professional experiences generally inhibits the corporate citizens from free and fair communications. Inhibitions are sprouting from pride and prejudices are influenced from galore of materialism. Materialism is a distraction that rather comes as a bonus if the path of corporate ahimsa is followed in letter and spirits. Humanity learnt during the childhood, college days, from world leaders, religious books and so on helps in losing the focus of the distraction of materialism enabling one to achieve corporate spirituality.

One is formally educated to obtain various degrees but informal character building happens when one grows from childhood to the initial years of corporate world. Do not have pills to have great memory, just a good intention should trigger the memory recall and follow the path of corporate ahimsa.

Forgive an offender just like that and experience a blissful good night's sleep. Just apologize for the mistake and enjoy a blissful supper. A blissful sleep and joyful supper act like a magic portion that has a cascading effect leading to a brighter career and being a good person with a sense of pride and satisfaction. Ahimsa as an attitude has these basic premises that have been experienced by everyone in the past and had never failed them. So why dread failing this time? Just go and do it without any regret. Corporate citizens adapting these basics will live a healthy life and there are other tangible benefits in terms of materialism.

Make sense of insecurity as a strength for corporate struggles and blend it with ahimsa principles and one will never regret.

- Expect nothing in return and you will never be disappointed. This golden line is written in Sanskrit, Greek, Arabic, Pali and so on. A lot of other golden lines that explained a great deal about ahimsa could also be read and understood in the right perspective. The main problem is what to follow: Him or His messages. Another issue is to read His messages as a believer or nonbeliever. The rigid rituals to read His messages had made educated persons disinterested in reading His messages. These messages should have been adapted as SOP but the mystery is best known to scholars.

In a corporate world, a lot of emphasis is given to the SOPs for good governance making SOP more relevant than the founder, but still the citizens bow for the founder than the SOPs. For example, the SOP of Microsoft is more important than Bill Gates himself, obviously Bill Gates will be more happy if his corporate citizens follow the SOPs. Head of the family make basic rules for his family to follow and his rules are more important than himself. Similarly His SOPs are more important than Him. There should be a choice to read the religious books as a part of religion or as a part of culture or as a novel thereby widening the scope of spreading the humanity messages making the whole world to live in peace and harmony.

He has created His humans ingrained with basic principles of humanity. The same is written in the religious book as a reminder. The adulteration happens in various phases of life. The main reason is temptation for short-term success. This temptation if avoided can make corporate citizen living a wonderful life and who knows the citizen while enjoying the life's bliss may be blessed by Him.

He lives in the heart of all human beings and expects nobody to break anyone's heart. The message is simple and clear. Follow it even if you do not follow Him. Believe in Him and read the religious books to believe in His existence. "God as a needless hypothesis" or "Free of Constraints You are the Universe" are diverse interpretations that are confusing but ahimsa as a basic human value is simple and without any kind of confusion.

Give ahimsa a chance in whatever logic it may come from. If ahimsa comes from religious books, reading or otherwise, one will find there is no conflict whatsoever at least in this principle. Cast love on a stone and write hatred on sand on a beach as after all it is not so difficult to do so.

There is no difference in believing Him blindly or His SOP or through exploration of nature, each path leads to eternal peace.

Believe in ahimsa, don't fight each other but fight with your inner self, blame oneself not others, curse yourself not others for perfect solutions. Meditate on Him for infinite energy and then miracles also look too small.

2 Believe in Your Destiny

Somebody born in a royal family is called as a good destined soul. How far is it true? Can anyone grudge a person for not being born in a royal family? Can someone differentiate everyone based on fair or dark complexion? Can someone with a short height and another with a better height be differentiated? Can some healthy person lend his health to a sick person? (Possibly no, except that a healthy person can donate blood or organs to a sick person.)

The word destiny is still evolving and could be researched on Google and still find that every decade a leading personality of the time has changed its definition. Who is better than whom is still relative and subjective. Is it possible to say whether a debt-free guy riding on a bicycle and going to office has a better destiny than a professional going to office on a loaned car? Or whether someone dies young has better destiny or someone dies older? Happily married person has better destiny or a singleton? A billionaire has better destiny than a millionaire? Philanthropist has better destiny than a pauper living on donations?

Leaders like Gandhi, Martin Luther King Jr, Mandela's destiny was better or their followers? Comparisons are plenty.

There are a lot of question marks, which still remain elusive for a proper definition of destiny. Without giving much attention to these question marks on destiny feel happy to be whatever you are. Make no judgments on materialistic possessions of others and be happy in whatever condition you are. Do not curse others that they are better than you, but feel blessed for what has been done well by you for the society.

A guilt-free sound sleep, a good health, ever ready for a divine smile, ever ready to help others, no grudge for other are few traits that can be termed as a good destiny. Trust in your destiny for these traits and you will never repent. Materialism is just a coincidence and it is not essential to be born as a good destined soul.

Good life, bad life, reincarnation and Moksha are a part of scholarly preaching. These are not still resolved for centuries and will remain so in the coming centuries. Trust your destiny in the simplest form and enjoy your life. Never ever try to compare one's destiny with others as one may end up demoralized. Define your destiny with a pride and do not try to live it with a fantasy. Just appreciate that to avoid disaster; just a few inches of extra run will help and a little sharpening of one's talent breaks the cycle of failure. Any failure to carry on this little extra effort leads to the wrong belief of destiny.

To know the destiny rationally, try to make a case study of the most popular song of the year, best actor/actress of the year, best movie of the year, best businessman of the year, best soccer team of the year, best airline of the year, best chef of the year, best orchestra of the year etc. The case study will convince you that nothing is impossible and nothing happens without hard sweat. Believe in yourself and your sincere hard work, you can change your destiny for the better.

3 Be a Good Corporate Citizen

Ever thought of yourself to be a bad father, a bad brother, a bad husband in a family? Off course not because of obvious reasons. As the head of a family one is respected for sharing love, affection and finances. Love and affection come from cultural heritage but money comes from the corporate exchequers. Although the money paid is for one's hard labor, it comes from the employer or corporate. As there is no reason to be the bad apple of the family, there is no reason to become a bad part of the corporate family. One has to be a good corporate citizen even for the fear of a selfish label.

There could be another reason than getting paid for the job to be a good citizen. Learning on the job and especially after making mistakes or getting success builds a knowledge bank. This bank has only a one-way credit entry having an interest rate of the knowledge deposits that is much more than the inflation percentage. The knowledge data bank needs a special care for the perpetual cleansing of dust accumulation by adapting ahimsa principles.

One is happy when the annual appraisal leads to expected increment or otherwise one is disappointed. The disappointment may be genuine but largely the comparative increments lead to dissatisfaction. There is a thin line between the disappointment and dissatisfaction and one needs to appreciate and be wary of. Selfishly, it is better be happy for the increment level without any kind of comparison if one has gathered sufficient knowledge bank deposit and still the credits are flowing in. If the increment and knowledge deposits are not to the expected level, then there is a serious need of introspection. Most likely one is a misfit and needs to upgrade one's skills or change the job. There is a possibility of hedging the gains or losses by adopting the ahimsa principles.

When the knowledge bank is overflowing, then the materialistic gains become obsolete and irrelevant. This may sound funny or impractical but a balance sheet of knowledge and increment will definitely give hints of lapse of the bank deposit date, which may be sooner than later. Remove all frustrations by counting the gains after the deposit. The deposit date will keep everyone guessing. Let this date be a pleasant surprise.

Imagine a situation when one is faced with betrayal from one's own family or country. Under all circumstances, one will not respond in a negative way, rather one will work on to correct the loose ends, and similarly, how can one betray the corporate world when it falls short of expectations. A good family man or a good national will always have to be a good corporate citizen. All characters are interrelated and any negativity in one role will have a negative effect on the other one. Be selfish and be a good corporate citizen.

4 Everyone Cannot be A Leader

There is nothing wrong in inspiring to become a leader but remaining a true corporate citizen and looking at the leader is equally inspiring. World leaders did not request their followers for their glorification but they inspire to push for a change. Change was achieved by followers making the leader successful and making their country proud. Accordingly, corporate citizens leaving their own leadership ambition aside play a positive role and will benefit the corporate that will eventually reward them proportionately.

There is much written on leadership and many books have been sold in millions but there are only a few thousands of corporate leaders. Corporate citizens have read a million books to get inspired to become a leader. Just talk to a few of these real leaders if they become a leader by reading these books and most likely the answer to the question would be in the negative. One concurrence could be easily drawn in reading the books on leadership and that is all the real leaders were good corporate citizens. A prerequisite for a leadership role is to first qualify as a good corporate citizen, which is in one's own selfish interest.

Aspire to be a leader, but not becoming one should not spoil the whole hardship of corporate journey. There are lots of people who consciously don't want to be lonely at the top and don't inspire to be a leader. Not becoming a leader is not the end of the world but keeping a focus on it to become a good corporate citizen makes one's career an interesting and a meaningful one.

Ahimsa principles help the cause. The principles learnt from cultural or religious values or maybe from world leaders act like a catalyst. A good memory of the past, like childhood, college days, perpetuates the desire to be a good corporate citizen and if possible may be even a leader.

5 One can Play A Better Role than A Leader

For a successful corporate, the success belongs to the leader or the corporate citizens and this is a chicken and egg analogy that has to be still solved. Similarly for conveying the messages of the God, the messengers were important, but equally important are those who followed and believed the messengers. Joseph and John believed in Jesus, Tapussa and Bhallika believed Buddha, Khadija and Ali believed Prophet Mohammad and Yashodha and Arjun believed Krishna. The messengers could send the messages of peace through these believers, thereby making the existence of the followers as important as the messengers.

It is unfortunate that most of the citizens want to take up the role of a leadership just for name, fame and wealth accumulation. Creed and desire are so overwhelming, it blinds the mind of the followers or citizens who should rather focus on real talent. The vision of the leader is best shared with the noble souls who become his first believer and this drives other corporate citizens to follow. These first believers are equally important without whom the leader or corporate would not succeed.

Although the corporate leaders are good communicators, those who convey corporate SOPs precisely, the demonstrations are best done by the leader's first followers to take it forward. The first believers spread the corporate SOPs or religion the same way the first followers of the messengers of the God and the history remains kind to the corporate first citizens as well. Divine SOPs have been conveyed to the messengers and their followers have learnt this and then spread it to the humans. This way the first followers of the messengers have made themselves into history and accordingly the first believers of the corporate leaders can inspire to be a part of corporate history.

The first believers of the leaders act like checks and balances for achieving the desired leaders' vision for the tangible success of the corporate and for a whole set of corporate citizens' welfare. It is, therefore, important that the leaders should first hunt for the first believers and the first believers should compete to become one.

What difference does it make to be successful or make someone successful probably by helping for the success of someone may be more rewarding because of selfless attribute.

6 Good Citizenship is a Way to Get Nirvana

Nirvana or moksha would not have a lot of takers in today's corporate world. Today's human race either believe Him blindly or don't believe Him but finds Him through science or some do not believe in Him at all. There is nothing wrong as long as one follows the law of the land for the sake of peace and harmony.

Moksha is to merge with Him and free one's soul from the cycles of life and death forever and live in eternal bliss. The meaning of Moksha could be simulated in corporate career as well and it may be in a real sense or simply a notion. In a real sense or as simply a notion Moksha; ahimsa is a guiding principle.

Moksha as a blessing does not happen accidentally and one needs to aim for it at an early career stage and follow the ahimsa principle. Repentance in the middle of the career can also help the cause but early stage focus can bring material gains as well and help achieve Moksha.

Another way of motivating oneself by remaining focused on Moksha is to believe that He is an infinite energy, as most of the religion believes so, and when one is aiming to attain Moksha by being in a career and when one experiences the infinite energy, then nothing seems impossible. At peace and at ease the thought of Moksha and the success of achieving it provide pleasures that no money can buy. The pleasures could be healthy life, satisfying family relationships, taking care of the next generation, balanced material pleasures, great social credibility and so on.

7 Doing Good Deeds is in One's Own Selfish Interests

There is no perfect lie and no perfect crime. Know this fact fully well and do not attempt any crime or corporate politics or lie about anything. One has a practical experience from childhood and college days that lie easily gets caught sooner than later but over ambitions erase this wonderful memory. This simple example eases a lot of unwanted tensions for the peace of mind.

Efforts required for attaining sinful pleasures or blissful pleasures require the same amount of energy. Possibly the guilt surrounding sinful pleasures is a tiring journey but focused energy spent on attaining blissful rewards is perpetually an untiring journey. The choice is simple to choose for blissful pleasures.

To do good deeds based on corporate ahimsa principles may require a lot of patience. Treading this path may have temporary setbacks, but it will never let you down in the long run. More so, it doesn't cost you a fortune, rather it shapes one's talent.

Divine creationism is based on His principles and if followed in letter and spirit will automatically lead to the path of success of blissful pleasures. One does a lot of compromise for attaining sinful pleasures and possibly less compromise for attaining blissful pleasures..

Any possible imaginary example will prompt or motivate all to be selfish in doing efforts for good deeds that leads to blissful pleasures even He cannot deny.

8 The Almighty is an Equal Opportunity Employer

Any country whether it is a socialist, a communist or a capitalist country has an HR philosophy of "equal opportunity employer." There is always a likelihood that the capitalist almighty following the path of socialism is likely to be an equal opportunity employer only.

Following the path of ahimsa ensures that good deeds are done and it is better than any average socialist doing lesser good deeds or any miser who is not following the path of ahimsa.

In all commonsense, He does not care if one follows Him or His SOPs but He rewards everyone equally for their good or bad deeds. His instincts cannot be different from the head of a family who gives equal opportunity to his offspring. Head of the family does everything right in an unbiased attitude. In every aspect, He has to be an equal opportunity employer also. Following the socialist path, He rewards the capitalist human who could be a corporate citizen as well. It is certain that almighty cannot be a communist because of obvious reasons.

Nature has a lot of beautiful stuff that is either appreciated or becomes an object of distraction. Both have a very thin line that all human beings are supposed to differentiate to make one's journey beautiful. The journey is called a life. A spice of ahimsa makes life fulfilling and it helps sorting out distractions.

Prayers are different for different religions for the same destination. Nobody is forced to pray but the spiritual deeds for humanity also lead to the same destination. Not reaching that destination means that the distractions have overshadowed the sense of appreciation. If one joins a corporate for an HR policy like this, then there are more reasons to believe Him as an equal opportunity employer.

Specially abled mortals have the right to complain but others have no right whatsoever. Is there any kind of doubt that He is not an equal opportunity employer having 99.9% biological similarities among the human race. Difference of color of hair or skin should not be used for discrimination. Don't ever doubt the self-belief or for that matter Him, just add the essential ingredient of ahimsa in the deeds for a beautiful corporate journey.